My Camel's Name is Brian

Jonathan Humble

First published in Great Britain in 2015 by TMB Books, the publishing arm of
the Tripe Marketing Board, a division of LEB Ltd, 57 Orrell Lane, Liverpool L9 8BX

ISBN 978-0-9573141-6-0

British Library Cataloguing in Publication Data.
A catalogue record for this book is available from the British Library.

Designed by Paul Etherington.

PICTURE CREDITS

Perils Of Courtship On A Windy Afternoon and Butterfly's Wing adapted from clipart;
Loyal To The End adapted from an original watercolour by Kath Tompkinson;
Sir Norman Wrassle/ Karl Lagercrantz, Wikicommons.

All other pictures and illustrations created by Emily and Jonathan Humble.

ACKNOWLEDGEMENT

The author is pleased to acknowledge the assistance of
Nick Broadhead and Paul Etherington with editing this collection.

DISCLAIMER

The author and publisher would like to assure readers
that no camels were harmed in the production of this book.
Any resemblance of characters who appear in this collection to real persons, whether
living or dead, is entirely coincidental.

Dedication

For Fiona, Emily, Jack and fellow members of the
Dromedary and Bactrian Appreciation Society ...
"May your humps be forever
commodious and free of sandflies".

Praise for My Camel's Name is Brian ...

Ian McMillan (Beat Poet)

"Some of this work is tripe and
some of this work is not tripe,
but even the work that is not tripe
is tripe of the highest order of tripe"

Mark Burgess (Author and Illustrator)

"Humble should display no false modesty"

Helen Perkins (*North-West Evening Mail*)

"wide ranging, inconspicuously thought-provoking and
undoubtedly very funny"

About the Author

Jonathan Humble is a deputy head teacher in a rural school in Cumbria. He's worked as a painter, lettuce picker and power industry engineer. Other than writing poetry and short stories, his hobbies include beard growing, pointing at poppies whilst saying "Oooo, they look nice!" and keeping the international coffee industry afloat with his patronage.

Originally from Goole in East Yorkshire, he occasionally writes under the pseudonym of Northern Jim and is rapidly establishing a reputation as the 'go-to' poet for fruit, sock and offal-based poetry. When asked about the intriguing title of his first collection of poems he replied "Can you ever have too many camels?"

His poetry has appeared in numerous publications and on radio. He appears regularly at Verbalise in The Brewery Arts Centre, Kendal and at other performance poetry venues in the North West of England.

Dear Reader,

Please find enclosed a selection of light and occasionally nonsensical verse under the collected title of "My Camel's Name Is Brian..."

Brian continues to be a useful if somewhat shy and elusive creature and he often lends a hoof when I get stuck in the creative process. Every poet should have one..

I should like to make clear the idea for a jet pack designed for cows is not one that's recommended by myself or The Tripe Marketing Board. We accept no responsibility for the subsequent inevitable disaster should anyone decide to investigate the possibility of developing a personal bovine flight device.

I hope you enjoy the poems!

JH ☺

Foreword

I think it was the talented Leeds FC midfielder and captain Billy Bremner who first said "A picture paints a thousand words". That being the case, you are holding in your hand the equivalent of perhaps ten or fifteen works of art, distilled into over 100 poems.

When the Tripe Marketing Board decided the time was ripe to appoint a new Tripe Poet Laureate, we cast our net widely and were delighted to chance upon Jonathan Humble. If, like me, you enjoy poetry that celebrates life and takes a light-hearted approach to socks, camels and pencils, then you will find much in this volume to savour.

Of course, there's plenty of tripe in it, too! I commend to you, in particular, *The Tripe Hound of Little Ormstonmere,* which is destined to become a classic for tripe lovers the world over.

I hope, after reading this collection, you are inspired to pen a few tripe poems of your own. I know I am.

Sir Norman Wrassle
Chairman
Tripe Marketing Board
Preston, Lancashire

My Camel's Name Is Brian

Are You Ready?

If on a quiet thoughtful night,
You pondered questions dark and deep,
That over years tormented souls
And kept the sages from their sleep;
Like what's beyond reality?
What is the point? Why am I here?
Why is my drawer full of odd socks?
Why do the English drink warm beer?
And who are you, and who am I?
And what is quorn when it's at home?
And why would people contemplate
The purchase of a garden gnome?
I have some answers I could share,
That might disturb the fragile minds
Of those whose disposition fits
The timid and more nervous kind.
So only read my further notes
Full in the knowledge what you'll learn
Could change your essence to the core,
Unhinge the mind and senses burn.

The Cumbrian Camel

The Cumbrian camel that dwells on the fell,
Considered by experts to be but a myth,
Is shy and elusive, but found by its smell
That wafts on the breeze in the realms of Penrith.

My Camel's Name Is Brian

My camel's name is Brian,
He lives beside my bed,
He has concerns about the ache I have inside my head.

Not everyone can see him,
As camels go, he's small;
In fact my wife and doctor don't believe he's there at all!

But being empathetic,
Dear Brian talks with me;
He tucks me in at bedtime and he makes my morning tea.

In many ways he's perfect,
I only have one grouse;
I do wish he'd stop leaving little piles around the house.

Question From A Supernumerary

I feel a little in the way, a nuisance I suppose;
I'm like a green carbuncle on a supermodel's nose.
A fly found in the ointment, a worm upon a plate,
A banker's contribution to a probity debate.
A vegan at a hog roast, a snake inside a boot,
The water lapping at the feet of mighty King Canute.
A politician's promise, a long forgotten vow,
As useful as a set of wheels and jet pack on a cow.
I feel somewhat superfluous, important I am not,
As vital to the circumstance as camels on a yacht;
And so I have a question, asked with due humility,
Within an endless universe, "What is the point of me?"

The Fall Of The King

O mighty hallux toenail,
Protruding and unbowed,
A king amongst all other nails;
So strong, so thick, so proud.
As legend, is your toughness;
You're hard, like granite rocks,
But now your days are numbered,
For you're wrecking all my socks ...

Dear Dorian Gray Enterprises

I bought an item in good faith about six months ago
Which has failed to meet the stated guarantee.
I have followed the instructions (to the letter I might add),
Yet the end result has disappointed me.

I positioned the equipment in the attic, carefully
And then left it to fulfil the task at hand,
While awaiting for improvement through reflected evidence,
'Though I am not vain you have to understand.

I have gathered testimonials, enclosed at your request,
To substantiate the lack of all success.
With the portrait now returned, a refund of the purchase price
Would be welcome at the following address ...

The Dance Of The Random Hanky

This universe of quantum doubt, quite prone to the bizarre,
Where oddity from time to time affects what one beholds,
Was host to washing on a line, with flapping handkerchief,
Wherein an elemental thought popped up amid the folds.

And speculating from its peg, upon a gaining breeze,
Along with shirts and pants and socks and other laundered gear,
It wondered what the view was like from up amongst the clouds,
When all at once the wind swept it into the atmosphere.

Within the summer air's embrace, in giddy loops it swirled,
Until its fresh awareness brought forth new found doubt and fear,
But then a lark flew by its side, at ease in nature's realm
And told it not to worry for the hand of God was near.

The hanky rose so very high and marvelled at the sight,
Of hilly fields, fine leafy trees and rivers flowing by.
It revelled with the friendly lark, who taught it how to dance
And joined in with its summer song of love up in the sky.

The other stuff down on the line, quite keen to have some fun,
Strained one and all against their pegs so they might get to go
And fly and jig and swoop and laugh up with their happy friend,
Away from all sobriety hard tethered down below ...

This universe of quantum doubt, quite prone to the bizarre,
Where strange event in random dream more properly belongs,
Was host to laundry in the air, cavorting with the birds,
With socks and shirts and handkerchief all singing summer songs.

Glad To Be A Dalek

I'm not your average Dalek,
You know the sort I mean,
All bent on domination;
Giving vent to all that spleen.
I like to think I'm different
From other Dalek crew,
Who keep emotions hidden
While exterminating you.
I don't agree with killing,
With plans to subjugate.
The Universe is lovely
And I find it hard to hate.
In fact, I've got my own plan;
I'm working from within!
I'm teaching other Daleks
How to knit and sew and spin.
I run a secret workshop
Where Daleks can relax
And find their inner Dalek;
Get the monkey off their backs.
We try to be creative;
To make things, not destroy.
I run a Dalek choir
Learning Ludwig's *Ode To Joy*.
So if you see a Dalek
In homeknit wool poncho,
Don't run off in a panic,
Come across and say "Hello!"

Never Meddle With A Faulty Tuesday

On an underwhelming weekday, Fred the Meddler volunteered
To embark upon a quest to find the man
Who, from sources of impeccable credentials he had heard,
Was responsible for Tuesday's faulty plan.

Having audited his inbox, with its plethora of mail
From a host of disenchanted, irate folk,
All complaining that this Tuesday was defective at the best
And in some cases "beyond a bloody joke".

This obliging, self-appointed, quasi-ombudsman set off
By balloon (as was expected by the crowds,
Who, with rousing and absurd rendition of *La Marseillaise*,
Sent him on his way up to the darkening clouds).

But while struggling to hold his course against prevailing winds,
Clumsy Frederick fell out from up on high,
Landing some would say quite luckily upon the scaly back
Of a dragon flying fortunately by.

After hurried introductions and apologies of course,
Fred requested that the dragon set him down
Somewhere close to where the architect of Tuesday's disarray
Had his office in the posher part of town.

But the dragon, feeling peckish (as it was around mid-day),
Flat refused to acquiesce to Fred's request
And without a by-your-leave, it scoffed poor Fred down in one gulp,
Leaving no time for the poor chap to protest.

Well the moral of this story is a little bit obscure
And one Fred the Meddler did not learn, alas:
Tuesdays often are a trifle disappointing I have found
And it's best to keep your head down 'til they pass.

Join In

There was a lad called Nigel Bates
Who used to irritate his mates;
He had this weird annoying thing,
A constant wilful need to sing.
Whatever time, whatever place,
A look would come upon his face,
Then Nigel would burst into song
And urge his mates to sing along ...
He could be out upon his bike,
Or in a match about to strike,
Whilst playing chess or sometimes bridge,
Or striding on some mountain ridge.
Upon the treadmill in the gym,
Or in the pool about to swim.
He could be in a chip shop queue,
Or even sitting on the loo.

It didn't matter where he was,
Or what the circumstance, because
When Nigel's tonsils felt the call,
He had to share his song with all.
But Nigel met a sticky end
While at the zoo, he did offend
A lion by the name of Leo,
Singing madrigals *con brio*.
And so the king of all the beasts
Was treated to a tuneful feast,
With little left of Nigel but
A song sheet with some teeth marks cut.
You'd think that with the end of Nige
No more with tunes he would oblige;
Yet as the funeral began,
Led by a solemn clergy man,
The mourners sensed a phantom throng;
As with the hymn they sang along,
Our Nigel's voice was clearly heard,
In post-existence afterword.
For with a good song in your soul
It's hard to keep it in control
And in a choir with angel's wings,
Forever Nigel sweetly sings.

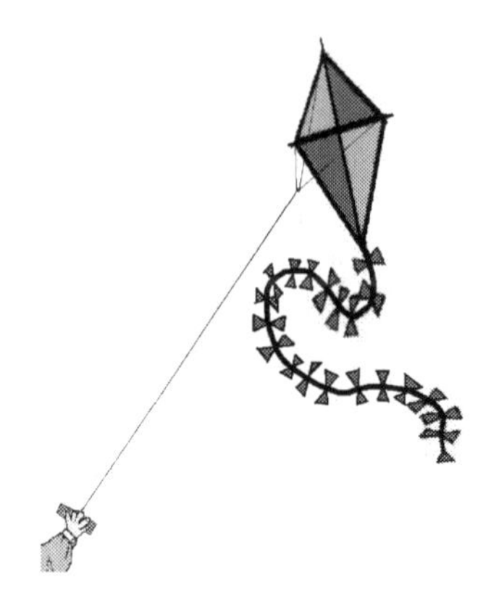

The Perils Of Courtship On A Windy Afternoon

"It's a big nose, I will grant you,"
Says the suitor to his girl,
On their Sunday stroll one autumn afternoon.
"But just think of the advantage
That our offspring will enjoy,
As they keep their feet dry during a monsoon."
Smiling kindly, says his sweetheart:
"It's a fine and handsome nose;
Aquilinity quite suits your face my dear!
But I do find fault, my darling
When the sun pays us a call,
For I'm in a shadow caused by your left ear!"
So in order that his girl can feel
The lovely autumn sun,
He adjusts his head one quarter to the right;
But unfortunately, as he
Executes this gallant turn,
Autumn winds take hold and blow him out of sight.

The Promise And The Reckoning

It crouched, but couldn’t guarantee
Its body was concealed.
It wondered what the cost would be
If it should be revealed.
Chased through the grass, through copse, by hedge,
Pursued without relent,
It knew of course they'd get the edge
Once they had caught its scent.
It travelled on, all wracked with fear,
A ghost by day and night
With watchful eye, attentive ear,
Heart racing through its flight.
Five years it had been on the run
Amid the hue and cry,
It hoped in vain that everyone
Might now just let it lie.
It tried disguise, to masquerade,
In vain in this regard.
It knew the price would soon be paid;
Hoist with its own petard.
And as it saw the line ahead,
Elections reappear,
The politician’s promise knew
The reckoning was near ...

Cosy

**You're in a kitchen by yourself,
The cosy's on the pot,
A little voice inside your brain
Starts badgering somewhat.
You do your best to be mature,
But then you find instead,
Before you know just what you've done,
The cosy's on your head.**

Recipes From The Happy Hippy Cook Book

A plate of scattered crumbs is set
Beside my comfy chair
And drowsily, I quite forget
Just who I am and where;
For something here is not quite right,
I feel it in my bones,
Which oddly seem so very light
For reasons unbeknown.
I find it hard to concentrate
On tasks of high demand;
My brain would like to relocate
To airy fairy land.
And as the mist descends to blur
An ever-changing scene
Of images more weird as 'twere
Dreamt up on mescaline,
A thought pops up amidst the bliss;
A mental note I make:
I must ask what my Aunty Fliss
Puts in her 'special' cake.

The Salford Sock Society

The Salford Sock Society has its meetings once a year
At a quiet public house beside The Quays
And upon the winter solstice, on the stroke of three o'clock,
They will each roll'up their trousers to the knees.

Using combs, they fashion hairstyles where the partings are quite low;
Just above the left ear, sweeping to the right
And with scarves around their necks to brace against December winds,
Later on they venture out into the night.

In a circle, in the car park, they all gather to revere
Items from the chairman's briefcase, fine and rare;
One red football sock with grass stains from a match in '68
And a lock from off their saviour's thinning hair ...

"Bobby Charlton! Bobby Charlton! Bobby Charlton!" they intone,
Pulling down their own right socks each one in turn,
Then the relics with great reverence are passed round one and all,
While the landlady brings tea out, in an urn.

With all tributes now completed, they adjourn back to the bar
To discuss Sir Bobby's triumphs heretofore,
Leaving free the car park for the yearly rites and rituals
Of the brotherhood that worship Dennis Law ...

Leaky Welly Blues

My raincoat is too big for me,
My wellies leak like mad.
With socks as damp as any sponge,
No wonder I feel sad.
The rain clouds seem to hate me and
A downpour now ensues.
I'm soaking wet and so I've got
The leaky welly blues ...
I'm not sure what a chap's to do;
Can someone help me please.
I'm so fed up I bet that I'm
More cheesed off than old cheese.
As far as weather forecasts go,
I seem always to lose.
I have no brolly so I've got
The leaky welly blues ...
The puddles gather all around
The ground is getting boggy
The rain has trickled down my neck
My underpants feel soggy
Can't wait to see blue sky and sun
The summertime I'd choose
For then I'd say good riddance to
The leaky welly blues ...

Postcards From Beyond The Looking Glass

I said goodbye to sanity one Thursday late in June.
I kissed it fondly on the cheek and gave it a balloon.
It soared into the clear blue sky under a gibbous moon.
I shed a melancholic tear and sang a mournful tune.

I parted from reality, after a pipe or two
And surfed across dimensions on a wave of Irish stew,
The recipe for which was told me by an old gnu,
In transit on a scooter to romantic rendezvous.

The first postcard I sent en route to Lunacy was dear,
I bought it in a Kasbah in a back street in Tangier,
From five performing oysters with a taste for Yorkshire beer
And all with accents from the county of North Lanarkshire.

They demonstrated how to knit spaghetti whilst asleep;
A skill that's underrated by the chaps who stick to sheep.
But 'though I practised, soon I found the learning curve too steep
And sadly was not able to achieve that quantum leap.

In Marrakech, engaged upon a deadly game of chance
With exiled semi-house-trained right wing cobblers from France,
I rolled the dice to win and leave the boot merchants askance,
As with a flirty cheese plant in a tango off I danced.

The last postcard was sent just as the cheese plant let me down;
She left me for some big shot from the richer part of town.
And at the time I thought that in self-pity I would drown,
But found salvation hiding underneath an eiderdown.

It's hard to unicycle with a duvet on your back,
And so I hopped the last bit quoting Proust, Poe and Balzac.
And with my fellow wanderers, met down a cul-de-sac,
Where we were told strife, woe and angst could all soon be
unpacked.

The terminal provided for the weary and confused,
Was furnished quite eclectically to calm and keep amused
The screw-deficient travellers, who wandered and perused
The waiting room in search of comfy chairs on which to snooze.

My life now is anomalous, with chaos everywhere,
But I've made most uncommon friends and what we have we share.
I spend my time with Baxter, an eccentric white March hare
And I am happy here beyond the looking glass somewhere.

... wish you were here ツ

Love Is Blind

Infatuation here behold,
A poet with his morning brew,
Compiling lists of similes
To illustrate his love for you.

He brings to mind your haunting face,
That none would say was bland or plain,
Which once observed, is always there;
Forever seared into his brain.

Round casements set below the brow,
Is how he now compares your eyes,
That like two bright celestial orbs,
Spin madly off across the skies.

And after past time childhood break,
Your traumatised and wayward nose,
Set in an artful Cubist way,
Now asymmetrically goes.

And when a laugh plays on your face,
Your ruby lips contort with glee
Like courting worms within a soil
Laced lavishly with LSD.

The poet drains his mug and sighs,
His heartfelt love now truly told,
His wistful gaze declares to all,
The beauty which his eyes behold.

Daydream

A disillusioned fifty-something contemplated life
One wet Tuesday while he mopped the kitchen floor,
Then he hung the floral pinny that he'd borrowed from his wife
Oh so neatly on the hook behind the door.
As he took the lid from off the biro deftly with his teeth
And the nib above the paper hovered close,
In his mind he tried to conjure words that aptly summarised
How he felt, avoiding clichés too morose.
'My esteem is sorely compromised; conformity's my all!'
Wrote this malcontent in ink as green as jade;
Then he left his note beside the tea pot with an added kiss
And walked out the front door horribly afraid.
With his brolly and his mackintosh, he caught the 42,
Which then whisked him off away and out of town
To a new life full of peril and uncertainty and risk,
With his rubric now completely upside down.
As itinerant and hired hand, he hitched across the world,
'Til he fell upon hard times in Marrakech
And while fending off attentions from a bearded chap in red,
Had a Godly visitation in the flesh:
"Hear me well, you lowly fifty-something; this is not for you,
With your mackintosh, your brolly and your angst.
You were meant for pipe and slippers, with a cup of tea in hand,
Not cavorting in a souk with mountebanks".
So the fifty-something thanked the bearded chap in red he'd met,
For his offer of position as a bawd
And he packed up his belongings with a wistful look around,
While his hand was taken firmly by the Lord ...
Then he found himself upon the lino, mop within his fist,
In a floral pinny feeling like a twit,
As his wife entered the kitchen, where she looked down to the floor
And informed him of the fact he'd missed a bit ...

A Dog's Life

With one ear flopped, my dog attempts my mind to mesmerise,
By gazing up with large and brown, pathetic, soulful eyes
And just in case I'm at a loss
To comprehend the scene's pathos,
Through mime his point is got across
With glances at his lead.
An epic battle comes to pass; for frailty he scans.
We hold our ground pertaining to our Sunday morning plans;
The slippers on with cup of tea,
Or outside sniffing every tree,
Which pastime will the outcome be
And who shall now succeed?
A stronger will and intellect this blackmail would outface,
Establishing that roles of pet and master were in place ...
The fact that now I'm in the field,
In welly boots my feet are heeled
And for my dog, a stick I wield,
Defeat, I must concede.

Extreme Northern Pastimes

Two aging, northern fellows met one Tuesday afternoon
At a quiet coffee house in Pontefract
And while dunking their biscotti in their macchiato froth,
Both decided that they'd make a sporting pact.

For they wanted to revive 'pig-hopping' as a local game
One of many Yorkshire pastimes full of charm,
Where competitors retracted either foot in headlong race
With a pig tucked firmly underneath each arm.

But unfortunately, as you know, the price of bacon rose
As the cost of living went on the rampage
Making purchases of piggies something one could not afford
If one's income was below a banker's wage.

So the aging, northern fellows in pursuit of goals and dreams
Turned to Plan B in enthusiastic mood
And they sorted out a set of rules pertaining to a match
Of wild ferretting at midnight in the nude.

The Pencil

The pencil wrote a learned note,
In which he dropped a Karl Marx quote,
So all could see his pedigree
In matters of great weight.
And by his side, awash with pride,
His chum the biro certified
In Garamond on paper bond,
His prowess in debate.
“We know our stuff!” was biro’s bluff,
Although, in truth, not quite enough,
For biro’s mind was unrefined;
Quite prone to blotchy spin.
And o’er the way, a rubber lay;
Hell bent on spoiling biro’s day,
Before the pair could both declare
A dialectic win.
“Your points are flawed,” the rubber roared,
As pencil sharpeners guffawed.
“And for a Bic, you’re rather thick!”
The rude eraser said.
A good retort, the biro sought,
But to his mind there came but nought;
In blotted ink, all he could think
Was “Go and boil your head!”
Then with a smile and bags of style,
The pencil waited with some guile,
For all ensuing ballyhoo
To cease and give respite
And as he spoke, with heart of oak,
Defeating foes at just one stroke,
With peerless wit, quite exquisite
The pencil showed his might:
“You've sharpened wood, ’til points are good,
Erased mistakes where’er they’ve stood,
But thoughts abide, unqualified,
Within this pencil case;

Do we agree technology
Could quite outmode both you and me,
With processed word quite undeterred,
'Til we are all replaced?
Come, let's be friends, as all depends
On how we now can make amends.
For lest we choose our wit to use,
The end I can foresee."
Then all around stared at the ground,
As thoughts became somewhat profound;
They'd not evade the moot point made:
2B or 2B.

Ponsby-Clasp And The Perils Of Peanut Propulsion
(or why chimpanzees avoid elephants on trolleys)

Come gather round and listen to a tale of yesteryear,
When men were men and went on expeditions without fear,
When handlebar moustaches were in vogue and hearts were true,
When shooting and then stuffing stuff was what we used to do.
The double barrelled brotherhood would travel far and wide
In pith helmet and khaki shorts to cover broad backsides,
As on their way through Africa they hunted high and low,
In search of the exotic; to the jungle they would go.
One noted bold Victorian was Gerald Ponsby-Clasp,
Renowned as an adventurer whose exploits made one gasp
And who, while at his club in town, declared his latest plan
To bring back to captivity a beast unseen by Man.
"I shall bring back to London Zoo that fabled pachyderm,
The greater spotted elephant, so that we might confirm

The truth in all the legends that its size is quite unique
And makes his jumbo cousins look like pipsqueaks, so to speak."
The other members all agreed his plan was quite first-rate,
And Ponsby-Clasp was made of stuff that made the Empire great ...
Six months then passed, as through the darkest depths of Congo Hell,
The expedition searched and searched, until they felt unwell.
Then finally, whilst trekking by the Tanganyika lake,
They heard a bellow so distinct, there could be no mistake.
And in a stroke of luck, the Behemoth that they had found,
For just a bag of peanuts, meekly followed them around.
It followed Ponsby-Clasp until they reached the Stanley Falls,
Where derring-do would see them overcome that water wall;
For Ponsby-Clasp decided they would build a sturdy ramp,
With trolley set on rails of steel, and beast quite tightly clamped.
A rubber bung was firmly placed to block its fundament
And peanuts fed, by barrel load, to fuel the elephant.
With careful eye for detail, a trajectory was planned
So that the flying elephant would in a strong net land.
Across the water on the other side and then to coast
Where in a steamer off they'd sail with what they prized the most.
But after months of feeding it, to generate the fuel,
No expedition member volunteered to be the fool
Who'd pull the bung from out the backside of the pachyderm
And so it took a while to get a chimpanzee to learn
To follow the instruction: "Pull the bung completely out!"
However, when unto the ape, instructions Clasp did shout,
The beast moved only bowels to disappoint the watching group
And shifted scarce an inch, whilst spraying all with peanut poop.
Then Ponsby-Clasp let slip the stiffness in his upper lip
And with great, heaving raucous laughter, seemed to lose his grip.
When asked what was the cause of mirth, he pointed through the dung
To where the chimp strove earnestly to put back in the bung.

The Cautionary Tale Of Fred The Ferret Wrangler

Fred was a ferret wrangler,
The best in Easingwold
And folk would travel far and wide
His wrangling to behold.
The gift was in his fingers;
The ferrets seemed entranced,
As hands and ferrets blurred as one
And to Fred's tune they danced.
But Fred had other passions
To complicate his life;
Across the valley, Cherry lived,
A chicken farmer's wife.
And 'though it was immoral,
The wrangler would pay court;
Fred flirted with young Cherry
Until husband grew distraught.
Forbidding Fred to visit,
He swore under his breath
That should Fred ever show his face,
He'd meet a pitchfork death.
But true love can't be stymied
And at a farmers' fayre
Where Fred's skills with his ferrets
Were on show for all to share,
The lovers reunited
Behind the produce tent,
Whilst ferrets, quite unsupervised,
On chicken hunt all went.
The upshot being carnage
With feathers strewn about
And chicken guts the evidence
Of carnivore blowout.
But those who read the future,
and entrails comprehend,
Would quickly have picked up
That Fred was due a sticky end.

And sure enough that Tuesday,
Behind his ferret shed,
The boys in blue of Easingwold
Found Fred completely dead.
Which serves as sober lesson,
One Fred did not discover,
Avoid the chicks when wrangling,
If you're a ferret lover.

Fat Man Jogging

A callow, handsome, cocky youth, with cheekbones, teeth and hair,
In black and white smiles out from photograph with scarce a care;
With baggy eyes and cheekbones lost and massive furrowed brow,
The older version wonders where the years have gone and how.

And so to find this long lost youth, he pounds the roads at night,
Preferring that his moving flesh is kept well out of sight.
Until the time the youth returns, his body he'll keep flogging;
What is that tremor that you feel? It is a fat man jogging.

Deplutocrat's Demise

Amongst the northern factories, a bob or two was made
By businessmen, in times gone by, when workers were ill-paid.
And in the Ridings tales were told of Mammon's keenest soul,
Who made the acquisition of great wealth his only goal.
Josiah Bowes-Deplutocrat surveyed his country pile
And on his sallow face allowed a cold obnoxious smile,
As he reflected on his wealth, accrued through dint of sweat
And broken backs of northerners he'd never ever met;
For landlord as he was to all the poor on his estate,
He gave no quarter when at times the rent came in too late.
The stories of his lack of image in a mirrored glass,
Like wildfire spread and were quite rife amongst the working class.
And on the rare occasions when through city streets he strolled,
The dogs would howl in fear, as in his wake the air went cold.
In every aspect of his life, he took without return,
Affecting those that wear flat caps, whilst lacking all concern.
Associates in business knew his grasping ways of old
And rumours spread he'd parted with his soul for Satan's gold.
For none recalled just how Deplutocrat first made his mark
And many wondered if his past held secrets deep and dark.
Then, on one inauspicious winter's day, a test was set,
By forces from Eternity quite disinclined, as yet,
To give up hope Deplutocrat had any soul to save
And cheat Old Nick, before he popped off to a wormy grave.
Angelic hosts would offer him the chance to clean his slate,
Forsake his wealth and do good works before it was too late.
But when in terms most stark and clear, the consequence was shown
To indolent refusal to reform and sins atone,
Deplutocrat was seen to sneer, quite loathsome to the last
And set his fate along the road to meet a fiery blast.
So, Providence, in unseen ledger, made a gentle note
And in its ghostly copperplate, this memorandum wrote:
That unlike Scrooge, Deplutocrat should not escape his fate,
And through excessive wine and food, his heartbeat should abate,
Until in death, Deplutocrat departed sans regret,
To sweat and toil eternally, forever deep in debt.

Poop Or Stick?
Being an illustration of Darwin's Theory of Natural Selection

In rhyming couplets here below, I set out Darwin's Theory
Of how Mankind developed from an early cousin's query:
For Monkey from the upper branches of his family tree,
Sat contemplating odds and sods and all things chimpanzee
And while he searched and groomed the hairy back of his best chum,
With fleas plucked with dexterity betwixt finger and thumb,
His apish mind reflected on the day's stand-out event:
Of how a stick applied in termite hole was time well spent.
"A most successful tool!" quoth he, and later on that week,
His kith and kin all brandished sticks like some high order clique.
Emboldened by this quantum leap in termite acquisition,
Old Monkey waved his stick about in crass triumphalism,
But as he swung it to and fro in careless, loutish show,
He caught a nearby cousin with a nasty glancing blow.
A prehistoric light bulb, with anachronistic glare,
Lit up inside Old Monkey's head pertaining to warfare;
His stick might be effective in a dust up with that group
Of rival chimps, and be more use than simply chucking poop ...
Quod erat demonstrandum; poop or stick's an illustration
Of Darwin's Evolutionary Theory of Selection.

The Very Little Thingy

"I should like to know the answer" said the very little thing,
From the box of unimportant odds and sods.
And the other stuff discarded, from below their layer of dust,
Trembled weakly as it argued with the gods.
For those deities of consequence, so awesome and immense,
With disdain looked down upon this also-ran
As the least important thingy in Creation now complained
That it hadn't been consulted on The Plan
"You are small and insignificant. You do not need to know"
Chorused all the high and mighty with one voice.
"Little thingies are more happy when in darkness they are kept
Living pointless lives with limited free choice."
So in order to disprove this thought, the very little thing,
With a barrel load of wit, aplomb and style,
Wrote a thesis stating deities belonged in fairy tales,
Then put down its pen and waited for a while.
Well, the mighty and mysterious and host magnificent
With self-righteous indignation and some pique,
Self-imploded in their anger leaving nothing but a smell
And a thingy best described as quite unique.

Sound Advice

In observations of the world, I find good sense is rare
And so sagacious counsellings I feel I should now share.
A life spent in pursuit of sense and order you will lead,
If this advice you take to heart in future word and deed:
I've thought about it hard and long, and feel I can now state,
That grasping nettles without gloves, I rather exprobate.
Experience has shown me not to spite my face unless,
I'd be content to slice my nose and leave a ghastly mess.
It's ill-advised to eat your hat, I've sometimes heard it said,
The flavour's over-rated and you often end up dead.
And if your aim is to avoid the spread of diarrhoea,
A finger in too many pies is not a good idea.

Fruit Fool ...

The kumquat sobbed upon the shelf,
A fruit somewhat benighted,
Despite the verse he sent his love,
His love was unrequited.
You see the fool was unaware
He'd got much too excited;
His muse turned out to be a plum ...
This kumquat was short sighted.

The Way Of Things ...

Lord Aubrey Danglewood was known by all below the salt,
To be a shilling less than full; a bank without a vault.
A chinless wonder bred from stock quite rare in the extreme;
His gene pool scarcely had enough to form a synchro team.
Yet 'though his lordship clearly was a bear of little brains,
His heart was true within his chest, and love coursed through his veins.

He loved his wife Drusilla, and his kids Hortense and Vlad;
He loved his hounds and horses and the servants that he had;
He quite adored the country pile his ancestors had built,
From robbing peasants after all their guts and blood was spilt.
His ignorance of antecedent slaughter from the past,
Was ended when enlightenment left Danglewood aghast;

Whilst watching on his telly, David Starkey blether on,
About transgressions of nobility from times long gone,
The penny dropped, and Danglewood felt deep regret and shame;
He knew he had to put to right the wrongs done in his name.
So there and then the noble lord decided to atone,
Renounce his titles, land and wealth and sell his lovely home.

He changed his name to Albert Wood and wondered how he might
Find ways to help alleviate poor workers' social plight.
His filthy lucre he disposed to swiftly give away
To victims of past Danglewood marauding and foul play.
He joined the Tory Party and became a candidate,
Returning as elected member for the Third Estate.

He took his seat as plain old Bertie Wood and set about
Reforming with a zeal in favour of those folk without.
But being dimmer than a twenty watt organic light,
The former lord became ensnared by Tory sybarites,
Who with corruption, greed, ambition, perfidy and sin,
Entangled poor dear Bertie 'til his mind was in a spin.

Despite his best intentions, all his plans were laid to waste,
And left upon his noble tongue, a nasty aftertaste.
He spent his days in Parliament, a journeyman MP,
Upon the backbench, quite confused, until aged 63,
His title of Lord Danglewood, by statute was restored
And wearing ermine, he was sent back as a Tory lord.

Now looking for the moral in this cautionary verse:
Decisions made in haste are rarely good and make things worse.
So Tories out there, if you wish to learn from Bert's mistake,
Protect your wealth, forget the poor, you've won in life's sweepstake
And comrades from the other side, this concept must be mastered;
Remember every chinless landed twit's a Tory aspirant hoping to make the Conservative A-List of candidates drawn up by Conservative Central Office at the behest of David Cameron.

Pontefract Postponed

While sitting by a tree within a wood last Wednesday week,
Perfecting transcendental yogic hovering technique,
A mystic would-be sky-pilot with pure unsullied soul,
Conversed with one determined to dislodge his aureole.
For pious Jim got chatting with Old Mephistopheles,
Who on a stroll to capture wayward sinners in the trees,
Discovered pure and lovely Jim, and thought it might be nice
To tempt him with some naughty ways denounced in Paradise.
Old Nick ran through the deadly sins, as impious tour guide;
From Avarice and Lust, to Envy, Sloth, Anger and Pride.
All swiftly were dismissed by Jim, with innocence intact,
Until the Devil tempted him with cakes from Pontefract.
"Where comest this fine black *bonne bouche*?" asked poor
demented Jim,
As Greed quite overcame his mind and left him in a spin.
A knowing smile played on Nick's lips, as pointing to 'The North',
He doomed young Jim to liquorice addiction from thenceforth.
That cake noir of devil's bush, it trifled with Jim's heart,
And drove the youth to madness cleaving sense and soul apart.
This innocent, corrupted by the Pomfrey taste and smell,
Had sybaritic urges, which he could no longer quell.
And thoughts emerged most naughtily of pleasures high in guilt,
So much that self-control and staunch resolve did quickly wilt.
To Pontefract went fallen youth in such indecent haste
To sate his hedonistic need for Spanish sweet root taste.
And there amongst the local folk, damned Jim was left to dwell,
On Devil's mission in the darkest depths of Yorkshire Hell.

The Tripe Hound Of Little Ormstonmere

Amongst the dark foreboding hills of ancient Lancashire,
The eerie howls rolled down the moors o'er misty peatland bogs,
To echo round the cobbled streets of Little Ormstonmere
And cause the good folk there to stare and shudder in their clogs.
For knew they well this howl from Hell and what it did portend
And how great loss was wreaked upon the town in times long past,
When from the realms of Lucifer, the beast's leash did extend
And Tripe Hound ran amok, to leave all mournful and aghast.
With sadness and reluctance moved the townfolk to the square,
Each citizen a-burdened with a tribute to the feast,
Which lovingly they lay upon a table by the Mayor,
Who checked its weight would satisfy and sate the evil beast.
Then from the hills emerged the brute with eyes aflame and cruel,
As townsfolk scuttled off to hide behind their bolted doors
And leave a trough of tripe o'er which the Tripe Hound could now drool,
And scoff the lot, before it disappeared amongst the moors.
No morsel left for Little Ormstonmerians to eat,
The town would have to live on offal served up in a skin.
With tripe now gone, and plans postponed for all to be replete,
Black Pudding topped the carte de jour and stopped them getting thin.
Amongst the dark foreboding hills of ancient Lancashire,
Satanic howls can still be heard o'er misty peatland bogs
And there behind locked doors the folk of Little Ormstonmere
Have cause enough to hide their tripe and shiver in their clogs.

Dear God ...

Creation is, without a doubt, inordinately large
And if you were to try to ask the Entity in charge,
Directly 'bout the most profound of questions in respect
Of life, the universe and everything, then I expect
The red tape and the bureaucratic paperwork would tie
You up so long, the odds are that before the end, you'd die.
Which, frankly, is an aggravation one could do without,
Deterring the agnostic from the path of the devout.
The option for the curious is: analyse the facts,
Extrapolate the truth from concepts formed in the abstract.
But riddles hang like 'why' and 'how' the stuff that's all about,
Apparently, or so the theory goes, grew out of nowt.
Big Bang from singularity or deity with beard,
Both lack the satisfaction of a problem nicely cleared.
I guess in truth the answer will remain beyond our ken,
Until all is revealed at End of Days, and so Amen.

BeardoMan !!!

The modern superhero comes in many shapes and sizes.
The skills these chaps display astound; they're full of huge
surprises.
The X-Ray Man can see through walls with true aplomb and ease
And Leapo Girl, who clears great heights, finds jumping such a
breeze.
Reflecto Boy can leave a room through any mirrored glass
And Super Cow's a bovine that produces gin from grass
But try to join their clique and it can cause procrastination,
This Pantheon of Greats is much averse to innovation,
The outlook of this super group's conservative at best;
Equivocation follows any membership request,
When the power of the applicant is based on something weird,
Like the follicles of steel inside our hero's superbeard!

Too Young To Die

There's a ghost inside my wardrobe, there's a ghoul under my bed
And behind the curtain lurking hides a zombie from the dead.
In the dark and dingy corner, watching with its evil eye,
Is a scary hairy creature guaranteed to horrify.
As I tremble and I whimper every night under the sheet,
Half expecting a most ghastly painful gory end to meet,
In the darkness, it is these words that I splutter: "God, why me?"
For I'm far too young to die yet, as I'm only fifty-three.

God's Gift

Three fervent bearded scholars, blessed with massive intellect,
Sat beside an open fire in debate
And the focus of their discourse, wrapped in finest silk brocade,
Lay upon a richly jewelled and golden plate.
For their god had tasked them jointly, as custodians in chief,
With the role of keeping safe His special gift.
So they talked and argued all night long of how it might be stored,
But their keen debate became a violent rift.
And as insult followed insult, with a push and slap thrown in,
Thuggish brawling from their discourse did transpire
And amongst the flying fists and feet, the present was displaced,
Ending up upon the embers of the fire.
Hosts of angels sent to oversee the scene looked on aghast,
As in flames their boss's gift was soon consumed;
For they knew that if a group of blokes, purported to be wise,
Bollocksed up the task, the human race was doomed.
As they fluttered off to Heaven to report the sad event,
Two were heard, in terms angelic, to agree
That the fault lay in the choice of which custodians to use
And that women were the world's best guarantee.

Tree

When as a spotty youth I sat upon that splintered form,
Outside the teacher's office with Bowes-Coleman, Joist and Lee,
I pondered on the question which the master had just set,
Pertaining to the odds of my employability;
What was my plan of action for the route that I would take
Next year, as at the 'World Of Work' I'd aim my shooting star
And had I finalised the sphere in which my range of skills
Could be applied so that I'd rise beyond the base bourgeois?
A lawyer and a vicar, politician and a vet
Had been considered briefly and dismissed with mild ennui,
But then a light most Damascene shone down and lit the way
And there and then I told the world "I want to be a tree!"

The Thoughtful Little Cactus

The thoughtful little cactus in the terracotta pot
Was a philanthropic soul with modest views
And while musing on the state of things upon the mantle shelf, She
would listen to the radio for news.

As an empathetic auditor, she catalogued reports,
'til she felt that something needed to be done,
'Bout the greed and the injustice and the nastiness she'd heard
And to try to make it nice for everyone.

So she wrote a manifesto with a view to sorting out
All the problems written on her little list
And she launched the greenest party that the world had ever seen,
To become the first Pereskiopsitist.

Jaded voters used to third-rate politicians and their ilk,
With their promises, their perfidy and spin,
In great numbers voted for the Cactus Party and by tea-time
Sacked the Government to let the house plant in.

Then the thoughtful little cactus from her base at Number Ten,
Set about improving everybody's lot.
And she proved a better leader than all those who'd gone before,
With it all done from a terracotta pot.

The Tragic Tale Of Sprout's Demise (being an explanation of the eating habits of some monkeys at festive times)

Before the ape forsook his tree, to totter upright everywhere,
There was an age, long past and gone, when sprouts had arms and legs and hair;
And in a world where IQ scores were running at an all time low,
The clever sprout bestrode the stage, proclaiming forth with fine *bon mots.*
And all the creatures were agreed that if poetic words were gold,
Their friend, the sprout, would surely be the richest by a good tenfold.
In admiration sprout was held by those who heard his words declaimed;
Except, that is, for one a little jealous of sprout's worldly fame;
For sulking in his tree aloft, old monkey felt *he* should be king;
To be admired throughout the land, deferred to by all living things.
And being of a nature dark, inclined to plot and stop at nought,
Skulduggery and wicked plan would be old monkey's first resort.
It wasn't long before his friends became aware of sprout's demise,
When in a nearby bush they found his legs and arms somewhat abscised!
Old monkey, questioned 'bout sprout's fate, denied quite flatly any part,
But gave the game away when he could not control a sprouty fart.
The rest is lost to history; we do not know what ends this scene,
Or how creation coped without their witty bard with leaves of green.
And many years have passed since sprouts could walk or talk of things sublime,
Yet many monkeys still enjoy a feast of sprouts from time to time.

Check Out

In fifty thousand years from now, from outer space in ships,
A set of archaeologists on interstellar trips,
Will land upon this planet Earth, from far galactic place,
To check out what had happened to the fabled human race.
Establishing how civilised the human folk had been
Before their obsoletion and replacement by machine;
They'll dig around for evidence of what occurred and how
Computers gained the upper hand in New York, Bonn and Slough.
And what they'll find will be revealed in strata rearranged,
Remains of human skeletons that over years had changed:
No lower limbs but casters which replaced their erstwhile feet,
A flattened cushioned pelvis that could double as a seat,
A single socket for an eye attached to scanning probe
And on the skull would be engraved a UPN barcode.
This evolutionary stripe upon Man's frontal bone
Would solve the case and make the answer well and truly known
The mystery resolved by fossil evidence in rock
And human race reclassified as 'item out of stock'.

My Aunties Come From Yorkshire

I have a lot of aunties,
A dozen rare and best;
They're spread around in t'county's towns
Up north, south, east and west.
These aunties are quite feisty,
Formidable and tough.
In times of strife their pluckiness
Shines out when things get rough.

A case in point is Rita;
Demure and introvert,
Ostensibly a dear old thing
In pinny and tweed skirt.
But aunty Rita's fearless,
Despite her dodgy knees,
She treks up t'jungle rivers
In her slippers, saving trees.

With thick prescription glasses
And loosely held false teeth,
She'll scale up t'steepest edifice,
Ignoring what's beneath.
For aunty Rita's famous
Within that SAS;
No foreign foe could lay her low,
Or make her acquiesce.

If wading through a swampland
And struck by t'deadly snake,
She'll give it what for with t'handbag
Then leave it in her wake.
She's part of Yorkshire folklore,
With daring tales abound,
A place where dear old ladies
Can amaze, shock and astound.

Behold !!!

A higher placed Authority arrived out of the blue,
Dissembled in a long white robe and sporting massive beard.
To say that I was shocked would be to understate the case,
For I was bollock naked in the bath when he appeared.
"Behold!" he said, with mighty voice "I come with joyful news"
And round the bathroom scanned as if unsure of the address,
Then spotting me within the tub, as for the sponge I groped
In bashful and quite vain attempt to hide my nakedness,
This spectre from some ancient testament drew back aghast,
With obvious embarrassment, he fumbled in his gown,
To bring out from some deep recess an old and crumpled note,
From which he read inaudibly, and gave an ancient frown.
"Apologies!" he said, at last and with a flourish grand,
He disappeared before my eyes to where, I've not a clue;
My only hope was that where're it was, the host he sought,
Was fully dressed and didn't have their bits and bobs on view.

I Am A Ginger Biscuit

I am a ginger biscuit;
I should be crisp and light,
But I feel somewhat soggy
'Cos I've been left out all night.

Mick And The Tree Of Knowledge

Old Mick the gnome, who loved to roam
And often wandered far from home,
Once on a spree, a tree found he,
Awash with luscious fruit.
He clambered high, for Mick was spry,
His hunger for to satisfy;
But knew he not, the fruit he'd got
Was biblical to boot!
"Oh clever me!" quoth Mick with glee,
Whilst perched up in the 'Knowledge Tree',
As high aloft, this fruit he scoffed
And spat the pips to ground.
Then God with might, and beard all white,
Brought down his foot from Heaven's height.
Acquainting gnome with all the loam
That layeth all around.

The Minister

How transient, the minister,
His life must seem to be;
One moment in the Cabinet,
In charge of you and me
Then in a flash, with foot in mouth,
A statement lacking thought
And off he pops to backbench shame,
Ambition come to nought.
But do not worry 'bout his fate,
He's bound to have put by
A tidy sum from those who shared
His love of corporate pie.

Anyone Seen My Glasses?
(The conspiracy theory)

How disagreeable it is when searching all around
For stuff that should be close at hand, and yet cannot be found;
The keys, the spectacles, the pen, the mobile phone, the purse
Are never where they ought to be within this universe.
And I shall tell you why this is, a secret known to few,
Which governments supressed, or covered up, 'til hitherto;
For there's a species yet to be identified by dons
Who work in anthropology and 'pooh pooh' eidolons;
A creature who can slip across from parallel dimensions,
To move and hide our keys, and quite deserves our reprehension.
This nuisance is without a doubt most devious and tricksy;
For those who do not know its name, it is the Quantum Pixie.

... (the truth is out there)

Tea!

In terms of elemental worth,
The civil and well bred agree,
That high in rank of usefulness
Is where you'd find the cup of tea.
For any low and downcast soul
The sight of steaming amber brew
Can lift the spirit 'til it soars,
Refreshed, to set horizons new.
And whether bag or loose leaf blend
Of Tetley's, Co-op or Earl Grey,
A well made cup of lovely tea
Revives, and sends you on your way.
So here I sit, with all I need,
In readiness at five to three,
With gingers placed on doilied plate
And teapot full of Rosie Lea.

Toast

In every household kitchen sits the humble toast machine,
A fundamental part of any culinary scene.
Ostensibly an old device for toasting breakfast bread;
You'd never think it could be used to converse with the dead.
Yet that's the tool the psychic friends of Odin utilise,
To contact those who've passed on subsequent to their demise.

This secret circle meet on every other Tuesday night,
To chant and dance in kitchens under eerie candlelight.
Then sitting round the table dressed in ancient Nordic gear,
One hand upon the toaster, begging Odin to appear,
They channel spectral energy emitted by each ghost,
Through those electric filaments more widely used for toast.

The Life And Death Of Egbert

A constant source of worriment was Egbert van der Pyes,
Who drove his poor distracted mum to premature demise.
The archetypal clumsy child was infant Egbert's style,
With spills and thrills and accidents recorded in his file.
There was in everything he did, an ominous portent,
As any simple task became a perilous event.
At Sunday school he was the cause of catastrophic blaze,
As during Candlemas with flaming orange God was praised.
With violin, whilst learning how to play and to compose,
He managed to embed his bow well up his teacher's nose.
And at an exhibition of some prehistoric bones,
Young Egbert tripped, to bring down Allosaurus on his own.
All through his life he stumbled at the edge of the abyss,
As chaos reigned about him, with bad luck his nemesis.
And yet, in truth, we have to note that through all this travail,
Our Egbert came out quite unscathed, to live all fit and hale,
Beyond the year three score and ten until, with hair all white,
He passed away, aged ninety nine, quite peacefully at night.

The Sad Tale Of The Reckless Rhubarb

'Twas on a clear and moonlit night in Castleford's green fields,
The stick of rhubarb's mind to thoughts adventurous did yield.
And turning to his nearby love, he made a solemn pledge
To sail away, like Hemingway and live life on the edge.
His love, a slender leek, was anxious for his safe return,
But with a brave and loving smile disguised her grave concern.
And pinned a white rose on his chest, that he might not forget
His roots lay in the rhubarb sheds of Yorkshire, not Tibet.
The rhubarb journeyed far and wide upon his reckless quest
And seeking thrills where'er he could from Goole to Budapest,
He soon became quite famous in the circles of those chaps
Who dice with death and thrive on courting danger and mishap.
But flirting with capricious lady luck, he soon found out,
How fickle fortune's finger of ill-fate can turn about
And duelling with a maharaja in the mystic east
Our hero was chopped up and served with crumble at a feast.
Quite unaware of how her love had met a sticky end,
The faithful leek made wedding plans whilst waiting for her friend,
But over years, in Castleford, the leek was left unwed
And sits in moonlight, quite alone, outside the rhubarb shed.

The Handyman's Flange

O Countess Angela of Troon, my lovely girl, my dear,
Although I know I shouldn't have the feelings written here,
For I'm the humble handyman on this estate of Troon,
Whereas your antecedal ranks sat on the stone of Scone.
Our love is doomed and we must never meet in furtive tryst
For I'm a staunch republican and you're a royalist.
Despite the dalliance that breached the unseen social fence,
I must to my side now return and live in deference
To what the world expects between the high and lowly born:
One life of high society; one life of muck and thorn.
In metaphor, my difficulty I would you acquaint
The way ahead will be a mighty test of my restraint:
The absence of your anchor and I'll find myself adrift;
With tap root severed suddenly my trunk will start to shift;
Your handbrake on my tractor made our joyrides feel so safe,
But once the cord of steel has frayed, the discs no longer chafe.
With loving words your handyman regrets to say, dear Ange,
My bolts of love must now work loose inside your lovely flange.

Herbert Loves Madge

I am a spotty Herbert, I'm standing in a queue;
I'm lined up at the pharmacy and clutching special goo.
This stuff has proved successful in bona fide tests;
A must for all visages with the stiffest pustules blest.
And standing at the counter, a few metres away,
The reason why I strive to cure this facial cassoulet:
Dissembled in a white coat and labelled with Boots' badge,
A smile for every customer; delightful, gorgeous Madge.

The Pasty Tax

O flaky golden pasty, how you trifle with my soul,
You're more tempting than lasagne, curried chips or casserole.
In innocence I pass by near the hotplate where you dwell;
As recepticals olfactic sybaritically swell.
And thoughts emerge most naughtily of pleasures high in guilt,
So much that self-control and staunch resolve both quickly wilt.
I reach into my fund of cash to sate this basic urge,
But find my eager fists without the wherewithal emerge.
Alas, alack and three times woe, I can't afford to eat
Your golden flaky crust that's wrapped around your tender meat.
Oh damn the powers that deny my gluttonous climax
And blast the coalition that dreamt up the Pasty Tax.

Why Pirates Dress As Pirates At The Pirates' Christmas Ball

Within a cramped and dimly lit, old, seedy, basement room,
Secreted in The Jolly Sailor Inn by Falmouth dock,
A meeting came to order of a shady little group
Of salty chaps with tricorn hats, big boots and stripy socks.
Bizarre in their appearance, round a table sat this crew,
Some members sporting eyepatches, with rings in mottled ears,
And perched upon odd shoulders, squawking out most noisily,
Were weird and scruffy parrots nestled on their buccaneers.
"Belay the noise and heed me well," the chairman bellowed forth
And glowered round the room at all the coves before his eyes;
"Apologies are offered from Black Jack and One-Eyed Sid,
They're currently a-swinging from their gibbets up on high".
"Oo arrrggh!" replied the motley crew, who downed a toast of grog,
In memory of Jack and Sid and all who jig and prance
When dangling from the hangman's noose on Tyburn's windswept
knoll,
Unwilling partners in Grim Jim the Reaper's final dance.
As silence fell upon the room and all respects were paid,
The chairman dabbed a teary eye and cleared his throat of phlegm:
"Good masters from the mighty ships that plunder Cornish seas
I call to order members for this Pirates' AGM!"
"Now as y'know, Agenda Item One, contentious be,
So we must full apply our best attention one and all.
A question of perplexity, that always causes grief:
What theme shall we 'ave this year for the Pirates' Christmas Ball?"
The group began a murmuring which quickly grew and grew,
As keen debate and argument erupted o'er the choice.
A fist fight briefly took a hold until a musket shot
Brought sense and order to the room and then up spoke a voice:
"We could all come as vicars," ventured Peg Leg Pirate Pete,
Whose mother dearly wanted him to get a clergy job.
"You scurvy dog! That's utter bilge!" another voice rang out;
T'was Peg Leg's mortal enemy from Bodmin; Long John Bob!

And soon the room became quite polarised between the two
For Bob's mates favoured dressing up as cowboys from the West,
With vicars versus cowboys as the choice before them all
A show of hands was how the question would be put to rest.
The chairman counted out aloud, as arms were duly raised
And taking note that those with hooks for hands had half a vote
Declared a draw and as was custom when the poll was tied,
A free for all ensued, with daggers drawn by each cut-throat.
And so like all the AGMs that pirates could recall,
This meeting ended badly with a mighty bloody brawl,
And as was customary in the county of Cornwall,
The pirates dressed as pirates at the Pirates' Christmas Ball !

Mrs Pottes, Can George Erik Come Out To Play?

When I was young I had a friend
Who people thought was round the bend.
At introspection he excelled
As in his mind he was compelled
To let imagination reign
And daydream rather than remain
Within his real and pressured life,
Where tests and targets caused him strife.
Now older, with a full grown beard,
George Erik Pottes grows ever weird
And from his somewhat hirsute mask,
With thick rimmed specs to aid the task,
He outward peers with some disdain
At all things modish and profane;
For from his odd trans-mundane view,
Surreally peopled by a crew
Of little chaps with pointy ears
Who gad about then disappear,
He sees quite through and well beyond
The modern face of this beau monde,
To places that the common folk
Would have to conjure or evoke
From childhood memories of the days
They spent in joyous abstract play;
With dragons, centaurs, unicorns,
Assorted elves and woodland fauns.
He sees them all, they are his friends
And have been since he turned the bend
Away from every rat race chore
And took the option to withdraw.

... Can George Erik come out to play Mrs
Pottes?

fun wiv foniks

i yam a likul infunt
oos lurnin howta reed
me teechurs wurkin veree ard
too elp me too sukseed
iym awlso lurnin ritin
and howta spel me naym
but foniks is kwite difikult
cos sownds int speld the saym

Where's That Thesaurus Mother?

That Roget was a clever chap,
Of that we can be sure;
His range of words is marvellous,
From common to obscure.
To say he's indispensible
Is niggardly, no less!
Most vital to each circumstance
Describes his usefulness.

I Had A Dog Called Grimsby

I had dog called Grimsby; a funny little tyke.
He wouldn't run to catch a ball, chase squirrels or the like.
He wouldn't bark at joggers. He hated to get wet!
He didn't growl or cause a fuss when visiting the vet.
My friends said he was boring, I ought to get a pet
With character, and lots of bounce, that played the clarinet.
But 'though he wasn't special, with Grimsby I would stick.
And so I thought what I would do was teach my dog a trick.
A skill that would amaze you, and build up Grimsby's fans;
I'd teach my dog to feed himself by opening tin cans.
And after lots of training to open with precision,
We got the chance to demonstrate his skills on television.
The outcome was tremendous. His fan base grew and grew,
Until it was quite difficult 'cos half the country knew
That funny little doggy, the one that opened tins,
And we were pestered day and night for autographs and things.
So me and Grimsby vanished, to get away from fame
And start a new life in a place where no one knew his name.
And now when neighbours ask me about my little dog,
Who sits ignoring squirrels, sticks and folk out for a jog,
I say that Grimsby's quiet; he doesn't prance or bite ...
Until my dog joins in the chat, looks up and says *"That's right!!!"*

Message From The Monkey

I'm not the organ grinder and I think it's fair to state,
That organ grinding isn't something that I'd advocate.
In terms of worth, this occupation dwells in lower ranks;
Remuneration's poor and grinders rarely get much thanks.
When on the street, engaged in preparation for a grind,
You often get abused by folks not musically inclined.
But worse than grinding organs is the role to makes them gape;
To sit upon the barrel organ as performing ape.
So when in thoughtful contemplation of your role in life
Avoid this choice if you're averse to poverty and strife.
As pastimes go, it's over-rated and I think you'll find,
That if you over-grind your organ, it could send you blind.

I'm Off!

I feel the pull from other worlds,
As in my chair I doze
And all it takes at ten past six
Is for my eyes to close.
Then through a wormhole I'll descend
And leave my mortal shell,
My essence moves beyond this sphere
To plenums parallel!

The Fool On The Hillock

I do believe I've heard it said,
Or maybe I have somewhere read,
It's ill-advised to eat your hat
Unless it's doused in butterfat.
Resist the urge to set your face
Or lose your head, and fall from grace.
For if you can't pass up a tilt
At windmills when the milk is spilt,
Keep out a well worn weathered eye
For any pie up in the sky
And don't, at all costs, play the fool
While sitting on a monticule.

View From A Tuffet

I'm not some timid relic
From ancient rhyme, all quaint,
Who when a spider comes to call, goes pale and feels quite faint.
In fact I like arachnids
That sit in webs and wait
For fat annoying bluebottles to land upon their plate.
I'm very fond of visits,
Foretelling cash to come,
From money spiders when I'm feeling poor and somewhat glum.
And as for those in jungles,
With evil deadly bite,
I'm fine, if they're on telly and my teddy's snuggled tight.
You see I'm quite courageous,
Not prone to girlie screams,
But there's one instance which can shake my manly self esteem;
For hairy booted beggars
Give me a funny feeling,
Especially when watching me whilst dangling from the ceiling.

Did you see the size of that spider's fangs ???

Confessions Of A Yorkshire Puddle Drinker

When I was six, I ran away
To far West Park, and spent the day
Amongst the trees, beside the dyke
And mucked around, as would a tyke
Quite ignorant of how his Mum
Would fret and most distraught become;
So much that neighbours searched for me,
A young and reckless abscondee,
Who when my mother's back was turned,
Went on adventure, unconcerned.
But then I found that I was cursed
With such a mighty unquenched thirst,
That off I set in search of cool,
Yet stagnant, nearby water pool,
From which I lapped like woodland elf,
Until, quite sick, I took myself,
Unsteady from this liquid feast,
Towards my home back in the east.
And after hugs and scolding both,
My mother made me take an oath
Forswearing outward bound mishaps
And always slake my thirst from taps.

Prayer Of The Primary Teacher

Deliver me, ye gods of fate,
From experts high on self-regard,
Dispensing judgement and critique
With OFSTED tick list or scorecard.
Take all these egomaniacs,
Ye gods of vengeance, I implore,
And seal them in a testing room,
To take the SATs for evermore.
And just to reinforce their angst,
Their flesh should be exposed to pricks
From hosts of little goblin beasts,
Who poke them with their pointy sticks.

The Cumbrian Ankle Biter

Within 'The Lakeland Walkers' Book Of Most Important Facts',
The hiker needs to know that ankle biters hunt in packs.
They roam around upon the fells in surly gangs of four
With nostrils flared to catch the scent of feet all red and sore.
And when the sweaty smell of socks floats on the fellside breeze,
The ankle biters gather in the boughs of hazel trees,
To plan their cunning strategies and isolate their prey,
Who stroll around oblivious along the green highway.
The only way to fend them off is with a pointy stick,
From freshly whittled local ash, all knotty and rustic.
And so to ramble safely this advice I'd not ignore:
Protect your ankles from this most voracious carnivore!

Don't Fear The Reaper

While on his way to harvest souls,
Grim Jim the Reaper paused,
As on the breeze he caught the sound
Of distant, well-fed snores.
And on a whim, despite the list
Of folk he ought to meet,
Grim Jim decided he should find
Which mortal was replete.
So through the woods and over fields
He strode, as on a quest,
To boost his set appointment list
With one he'd mark as 'guest'.
And in a clearing, by a stream,
The soul to be deceased,
A plump and comely maid asleep,
Snored by her campside feast.
Yet as he raised his scythe aloft
To send her on her way,
A strange unheard of thing occurred
To ruin Jim's whole day:
Distracted by her lovely face,
His heart gave out a beat,
Which for a long dead organ
Was a most unlikely feat.
And in this state of mortal lust,
His loose held scythe fell free,
To cleave from shoulders
Jim's own head; a grim decapitee.
And so the reaper reaped himself,
To join his list of dead ...
Which proves that sex at work is bad,
If you're to keep your head!

The Luggerbug

The greater spotted luggerbug,
Less welcome than the common slug,
Frequents aristocratic hair
Of minor royals in Finisterre
And has a talent seldom seen
In parasites high on hair cream,
As from within the coiffeured curls,
Amongst the rubies and the pearls,
It sings a snatch of Spanish tunes
To Latin rhythms on the spoons,
Which drives the upper class insane
Upon that north west point of Spain.

Here's One I Made Earlier

I look at you.
You look at me.
Your eyes reveal a heartfelt plea.
The egg that's smashed,
Now oozes out
Upon the kitchen tiles and grout.
You sweep a beat
With rhythmic rear
And cock a hopeful floppy ear.
My heart; it melts,
As from your nose,
A dewdrop dangles unopposed.
I step away,
As herebefore,
The mess is lapped up from the floor.
The service done,
With willing tongue,
I start again my egg fooyung.

Ballad Of The Fruit Bowl

The speckled ripe banana lay alone inside the bowl
And worried 'bout the consequence for his immortal soul,
Because he'd sung his friend, the pear, an optimistic ballad
Two minutes 'fore she was chopped up as part of a fruit salad.
He wondered if he'd let her down, because in him she'd trusted;
Oblivious to his own fate, as he was doused in custard.
And so we learn that optimism in the bowl of life
Is hopeless, once the Chef decides to wield the salad knife.

Nightmare!

There is a dream I have at night,
It's witnessed from afar,
In which momentous world events
Include my avatar.
This second me will get involved
In solving major issues,
My *doppelgänger* cures the cold,
So there's no need for tissues.
He strides across the Middle East,
Removing all dictators,
Then liberates ill-gotten gains
From bank manipulators.
He sorts out eco-problems
And explains the Universe,
So Einstein can complete his work.
But then it all gets cursed,
As all this work for good
Is put to question and the test.
Why is he semi-naked,
Dressed in underpants and vest?

Determinism In The Kitchen On A Sunday Morning
(the butty poem)

Apologies to all my veggie friends and those alike,
On Sunday mornings on the stroke of ten, the urges strike
And gravitating to the fridge, I find myself en route,
The object of my foraging is not some healthy fruit.
More basic instincts take a hold and freewill turns to putty,
Despite my best-laid diet scheme, I make a bacon butty.

Jolly Fred and the Ministry of Happiness

Fenella had a husband who was known as Jolly Fred.
His hobby was collecting stuff and potting in his shed.
He always had a cheery word and all his neighbours said :
"He's such a happy chap!" as he sped by on his moped.

Then one day on the radio, Fred heard the newsman say,
The government had got a plan to measure everyday
The happiness of citizens, who all must now obey
And meet their targets joyfully; be gay without delay.

Now under this external glare, Fred felt quite insecure
And dear Fenella saw her husband change from something pure,
Into a man whose humour failed with little chance of cure;
And Fred became quite sullen with an outlook rather dour.

Despite the fact that elsewhere something jolly good had died,
The Minister of Happiness declared with glowing pride:
"Statistics show an upward trend that cannot be denied!"
And MPs left the Commons feeling jolly satisfied.

In act of desperation, Fred and Fen escaped away
To some place where the government had very little say.
They lived their lives contentedly, without the men in grey
And no more damned initiatives or targets of the day.
... Hooray!

When I Grow Up ...

"I am only very little," said the very little thing,
While it looked up at the big things from below.
"And I do wish I was bigger so I might reach all that stuff
That I can't reach lest I go on tippy-toe.
If I eat up all my veggies and I'm early to my bed,
Then I'm told that very soon I'll start to grow!
But I do hope that it happens sooner, rather than too late,
'Cos I'm wrestling next week in my first Sumo!"

Fred The Toad

I had a pet called Fred the Toad,
He wasn't very jumpy.
I let him play upon the road
And now he's flat, not lumpy.

My Guilty Secret

I know a naughty fellow,
Who has a secret vice.
He keeps it from his family, which really isn't nice.
When shopping with his dearest,
Mid-morning, Saturday,
He surreptitiously awaits the time to slink away,
Then lurks around in shadows
And nips inside, as off he
Takes twenty minutes for himself, to slurp a Costa coffee.

The Musings Of A Mollusc

I slither as a lowly slug
And wonder what I've done
To warrant this ignoble stage
Of incarnation fun.
In past lives I've tried hard to please
All those I've met and known;
My testimonials all state
The qualities I own.
'Sincerity' and 'Honesty'
Were oft' my middle names,
So much that folk would come to me
For advice o'er again.
Now, as a humble mollusc
In this place I reign supreme.
These marigolds and hostas
Are the stuff of sluggy dreams.
The gardener's hope of red rosettes
I dash with ruthless streak,
With future 'Best In Show's all doomed
And eaten in a week.
And on my unctuous journey
All I do is wreck and munch;
The holey progress of my route,
A record of my lunch.
So now I'm here in this veg patch
In slimy slug condition.
It's quite a change from my last job;
A former politician.

Oink Oink!

When I was young and spotty, and my ears were somewhat wet,
If told, “the Moon is made of cheese!” wide eyed was what I’d get.
But now that I am ancient and much wiser, I suppose,
A revelation of this type I treat with more repose.
A sceptic is what I’ve become; a classic Pyrrhonist.
Unless it’s witnessed with my eyes, it’s usually dismissed.
I don’t believe in fairies, Peter Pan can sling his hook,
At every rainbow's end all that you’ll find’s a crock of muck.
We haven’t had a visit from beyond the stratosphere;
All talk of small green aliens is idle chat I fear.
Intelligent design’s a dodgy concept with much fault.
The idea of omnipotence I take with pinch of salt.
And when a politician signs a pledge before ‘The Press’
And says with great sincerity: “To remedy this mess,
I promise the electorate, without a word of lie ...”
... An image jumps into my mind wherein a pig might fly.

The Voice

Obsessively, compulsively,
I check on every door.
The windows are all firmly locked,
The fire is no more.
The fridge is shut, the gas is off,
I hear no dripping tap
And every plug is out,
Thereby avoiding a mishap.
I've made sure all the lights are out,
It's nearly time to go.
Appliances in every room
Are sorted now, and so,
I reach the front door hopeful that
The house is safe, but then,
A voice inside my head says:
"Now go check it all again!"

The Tale Of The Tonsorialist

As Taras Bulba's barber,
I'm always paid in cash
To keep in trim, the Cossack way,
His top knot and moustache.
Beyond the Ural Mountains
This cut is fairly rare
And chaps these days have other ways
Of styling facial hair.
But if you come to my shop,
You could end up a winner!
Whatever style you enter with,
You'll exit like Yul Brynner.

The Haggis Botherer

Beware the haggis botherer,
It lurks where none can see
And bides its time quite patiently,
Be-sporraned near Dundee.
It stalks its prey most doggedly
And tramps the purple heather,
In wellies worn below the knee
In dreadful Scottish weather.
The haggis grazing in the wild,
No notion of its fate,
Will chomp away quite merrily,
Until it's all too late.
In blur of knee and sporran
Ends this tale of life and death
And amidst the lowland drizzle
Haggis takes its final breath.
But botherers are rare now,
Their prey is often farmed.
And numbers are adwindling
To naturalists' alarm.
So be aware you tourists
Of haggis sold in shops,
You might be taking food away
From baby botherers' chops.

Bowling With Dad

When bowling down at Morecambe,
With Mum and Em and Jack,
Old Dad has to be careful
'Cos he has a dodgy back.
Then once the game gets going,
Old Dad forgets the pain
And competition takes a hold,
His joints cope with the strain.
But as the points get closer
The outcome feels uncertain
And when Old Dad tries just too hard,
His back goes for a Burton.

... Silly bugger!

Not Really

There's nothing I like more
Than standing in a queue
And watching all the other tills speed up to get folk through.
Or walking with the dog
And throwing him a ball
Which he ignores to chase some sheep by leaping o'er a wall.
I take delight, you know,
In every crowded place
Where strange assorted weirdos meet to fill my personal space.
And my idea of fun
Is listening to some bloke
Who's privvy to God's plan for me some time after I croak.

The Traveller's Tale

When I was young and fluffy,
And my bow a lovely blue,
I'd spend the days with other toys
And play was all I knew.
The world outside was hidden,
Until I lost my eye.
I thought a patch would do the trick;
A pirate's life I'd try.
But when your fur goes missing
And your stitches come undone,
To little Jim or Celia
You cease to be much fun.
My playroom days were numbered,
I sensed the doom within.
By Christmas it was time to go
Into the rubbish bin.
However, dearest reader,
Don't worry or feel sorry,
I've seen the world, tied to the grille
In front of this bin lorry!

Pips ...

Alas, alack and three times woe,
We have a stark imbroglio;
The Greenwich 'pips' intermezzo
Is absent from the radio.
How will they cope with this dead-air
In breezy Weston-super-Mare,
Enduring pregnant pauses where
The friendly pips would once declare?
But do not get all woebegone,
Re-starch that upper lip, my son,
The British phlegm flows from hereon,
Let's all keep calm, and carry on!

(Rule Britannia ... etc.)

Save The Twerp

In contemplation of the world,
With all the change and all the doubt,
I reminisced on times gone by
And went on mental walkabout.
I pondered on the ‘common twerp’,
Who seem these days so awfully rare;
One used to see them all the time,
In search of misplaced savoir faire.
In past times with their witless ilk,
The ‘nitwit, ‘barmcake’ and the ‘fool’,
You’d see these chaps make endless gaffes
And be the butt of ridicule.
But wait a mo’, who are those boobs
Appearing on my old TV?
It’s Michael Gove and Edward Balls;
A brace of gormless ‘twerps’ I see.
Thank goodness that we have ‘The House’;
A place of refuge for that group,
Where ‘twerps’ and ‘fatheads’ congregate,
With other types of ‘nincompoop’.

Quantum Theory According To Camels

I bought some quantum wellies,
Which felt quite expeditious,
But, as a consequence, my life's become somewhat capricious.
I cannot plan in detail,
That would be too ambitious,
For now I find most outcomes tend to end up as fictitious.

Who Ate All The Pies ?

The fine exquisite savoury upon this Wedgewood plate,
With silvered foil encasing chunky meat and tasty crust;
A culinary pinnacle from ancient recipe,
To which the passing years our master British chefs entrust,
Is much desired and coveted by gourmets of the world,
Who wail and gnash their teeth and weep full buckets from green eyes,
Dejected in the knowledge that across the oceans deep,
We make upon this sceptred isle, the King and Queen of Pies.

... (And tourists' feet in ancient times
Walked upon Lakeland's mountains green:
And with a pork pie in both hands,
Were there on England's pastures seen!)

Elegy For A Tick

The tick that has adhered itself on to my inner thigh,
Reminds me of those bold adventurers from times gone by,
In ticky terms, a Shackleton, or Edmund Hillary,
It plots its route from base camp round the back of my right knee,
Despite the brave tenacity with which it grips my skin,
I fear its days are numbered and it's destined for the bin.
I can't help but admire its stout refusal to succumb,
But that won't save it ending up between finger and thumb.

Loyal To The End ... Of The Sandwich

My dog, who sits obediently beside this comfy chair,
His canine eyes epitomise intense and loyal trust,
Ostensibly is focused on his master's every move,
But is in fact observing an uneaten jammy crust!

Spread The Word

Geoffrey Augustus Barabas the Third
Decided he wanted to spread the good word
And in his epiphanal state he set out,
Declaiming effusively like one devout.
He went on a visit to see his good friend,
Cordelia Bottle, who lived round the bend.
They talked all day long and for half of the night,
Until dear Cordelia saw a bright light.
"Hosanna! Eureka! I've got it," she cried.
"I see what you mean and it can't be denied!"
And now with a zeal the good word these two spread,
That Marmite and Sunpat are Heaven on bread.

107 Weatherill Street

In fundamental basic lore,
O'erlooked by scientific types,
The centre of the Universe
Was where my Grandad kept his pipes;
Set by his battered best armchair
In regimented rack of oak,
All present and in readiness
For tales told through a whirl of smoke.
And there we'd sit, old man and boy,
As in the grate the coal fire burned,
In shared adventure through his words,
Whilst all around Creation turned.

Mid-Life Crisis

I'm fifty and I'm overweight, my best years have gone by.
I hanker for the days when as a youth my feet could fly;
Gymnastic skills came easily to one who was so lean,
But now my waistline measurement has gone beyond obscene.
I want to do a cartwheel, execute a back handspring
And fly with double somersault; a bird upon the wing.
I'd love to do a pirouette and hold an arabesque,
A muscled leg inclined behind, without looking grotesque.
I wish I was more supple, acrobatic, lithe and fit,
But in this frilly leotard, I look a proper twit.

Scientifically Reversible Processes

It rained and rained, then rained some more,
'Til all the world was boggy.
My hair was wet, my socks were damp,
My underpants felt soggy.
But when the sun began to shine,
It warmed all rained-soaked creatures;
Evaporation took effect
And dried our dampened features.

A Butterfly's Wing

While Rufus Rat was dining in the bin of an MP,
He little thought how disingenuous his host could be,
Because the lexicon of Rufus lacked his perfidy.
When Cough the cat ate up this rat all lousy with the fleas,
She little thought the rat she'd caught was riddled with disease,
Contracted from descendants that belonged to Socrates.
When Dick the dog barked at poor Cough last Tuesday afternoon,
He little thought she was the pet of Cedric, Duke of Troon,
Who'd died that day whilst running with a mouth crammed full of
spoon.
When Bob the boy had teased the dog en route to Sunday school,
He little thought his actions symptomatic of a fool,
He should have spent his Sundays on the fells in a cagoule.
When Alice, aunt of Bob the boy, kissed said boy on the cheek,
She little thought with rancid garlic smell her breath did reek,
Which planted images in young Bob's mind of fenugreek.
When Dave the MP listened to Aunt Alice's complaint,
He little thought how damaged was his image for restraint,
When newspapers displayed him wearing fishnets and face paint.
The lives we lead are linked 'ere we be cabbage or be king,
Our action and intention can affect 'most everything
And hurricanes are sometimes caused by beat of insect wing.

Lament

"What is that awful rancid smell?"
I hear them say outside,
As deep within this cold dark place,
I sit and think and hide.
Ashamed I am and quite alone,
My self-esteem is low
And if I'm ever found in here,
Into the bin I'd go.
Abandoned, lost, left on the shelf,
Unloved and gone to pot;
A furry growth, my overcoat
(The bit the cook forgot).
I'm mouldy tripe; gone off, gone bad,
My sell-by date's gone by.
A stinky mess is all I am;
Not fit to boil or fry.
Behind the butter and the ham,
I know my time is short;
I doubt I'll end up in a dish
Of tripe stuffed goose with port.
I'm mottled green and past my best.
My taste is quite obscene.
I'll never now be part of any
Tripey haute cuisine.

The Gurgle

There's a place inside our bathroom
Which is damp and full of gunge;
It is where the Urgle Gurgle eats
The shampoo, soap and sponge.
I'm convinced it's had Dad's toothbrush
(He's been brushless for a week)
And my plastic duck has disappeared;
It went without a squeak.
In the spot where Mum's leg razor was,
There's just a soapy space.
And the bath-cap that my sister wears
Has gone without a trace,
Where my Granny put her false teeth
Is a first class mystery,
But my guess is that the Urgle Gurgle
Ate them for its tea.
For the clues are there for all to see
If you should care to look,
With prints found round the bathroom
From its claws all caked in muck.
The Gurgle lives and eats
Within the basin over-flow.
I have seen its filthy features
As I've washed my face, and so,
I advise you all to keep clear of
This strange and hungry creature.
By the way ... has anybody seen
My dear old Aunty Rita?

I Am An Archers' Addict

I have a little problem
With which I am afflicted;
There is a Sunday omnibus
To which I am addicted.

I should be outside digging,
Or weeding in the garden,
If I'm to rival Monty Don
In my wife's heart's affection.

But rather than be useful,
I'll make a bacon sandwich
And brew a pot of morning tea,
Whilst tuning in to Ambridge.

Then on my favourite armchair
I'll settle nice and comfy
And find myself sinking a pint
With my mate Eddie Grundy.

The Mind Of God

So, there I was just thinking things about the Universe,
Of how the plight of humankind has gone from bad to worse.
I'm feeling sort of lonely here, my confidence is low,
My self-belief is waning too, perhaps it's time to go.
And then I hear from Hawking,
A fact that makes me weary;
Omnipotence and Grand Design's been ousted by M-Theory.
And what along with Dawkins,
Who says I'm a delusion,
I find that I just can't escape the natural conclusion.
It's time for Me to exit, hang up my lightning rod.
It's up to you to sort it out,
I've had enough ...
Bye ... God.

There Was A Merchant Banker

I found myself recoiling at a banker's unctuous tone
That wafted through the airwaves from my radio today,
Bemoaning the injustice of a bad press for his ilk,
Defending the enormity of city bankers' pay.
I wondered at my feelings of revulsion for this chap;
Was this some knee-jerk, class-based jealousy or personal quirk?
I wrestled with my conscience as I pondered deep and hard,
Concluding that in fact this banker was indeed a berk.

... and first against the wall, come the revolution.

Ode To A Bagpipe Weevil

When asked to share the secret how
It tolerates that grating whine,
The bagpipe weevil will reply:
"By my watch, it is half-past nine!"

Goolie

I'd like to be a man of taste,
An all round connoisseur,
Who'd spellbind any audience
As witty raconteur.
My aim is to be seen as wise,
Experienced, concise,
With contacts high in politics
Who'd seek my best advice.
I'd like to be a dilettante
Sophisticated, cool,
But it's not easy when you are
A boring git from Goole.

Beware Of Spoons

As Jim sat in the kitchen,
One Tuesday afternoon,
He let his mind drift aimlessly,
While gazing at a spoon.
The strange distorted features,
That stared back at his face,
Grew angry and affronted
By Jim's lack of social grace.
And grabbing our poor hero
Quite roughly by the ear,
The image pulled Jim off his chair,
Beyond our mortal sphere.
And left upon the table,
That Tuesday afternoon,
No clue to Jim's new whereabouts,
Except a bloody spoon!

The End

As we approach 'The End Of Days' and hope becomes despair,
Remember what the wise man says and find fresh underwear.
You will not find advice more sound, insightful or germane,
As inextricably all that we know goes down the drain.
For as the Maker waits for us beyond this mortal sphere,
She will not well appreciate the remnant smell of fear.
Resist the urge to run and scream, as headless as the rest.
Go placidly amid the noise in clean socks, pants and vest.

Made in the USA
Charleston, SC
09 February 2015